Office 2019 for Beginners

The Premiere User Guide
for Work, Home & Play.

Cheat Sheets Edition:
Hacks, Tips, Shortcuts & Tricks.

Standard Ordinary Human

Solutions & Training, 20-year Microsoft Veteran

Office 2019 for Beginners

Release: 2.2.15.7

Table of Contents

About Ordinary Human

Ordinary Human is a 20-year veteran of Microsoft who previously worked with various Microsoft teams to write documentation for Windows, Windows Server and other Microsoft products. If you have ever used any Microsoft product or operating system or had Microsoft training, you've probably seen Ordinary Human's work in action.

Ordinary Human pledges to update this manual from time to time to make corrections and changes as Office 2019 changes, and to add content. How much time Ordinary Human can dedicate to the book depends on its readership and participation from readers like you.

Introduction

When it comes to technology and computers, ordinary humans often need a little help getting through the day. Sometimes ordinary humans wish training manuals had just the steps needed to get the job done and that's exactly what you'll find in this handy quick reference guide filled with step-by-step instructions and shortcuts for how to use Microsoft Office 2019.

Not only does this book provide a streamlined and concise learning experience, it is also an easy to use reference guide for any type of user that will help you get the job done quickly. Using this guide, you'll be able to:

- Teach yourself the essentials and latest features
- Learn how the new Office works
- Work more efficiently with Office 2019
- Find just the tasks you need

Flying Start

Throughout this guide, where we use CLICK, RIGHT-CLICK and DOUBLE-CLICK, you can use the touch equivalents of TAP, PRESS AND HOLD and DOUBLE TAP. HOVER means to position the mouse over the designated item without CLICKING.

When working in Tablet mode, CLICK START should be replaced

with CLICK ▤ on the START screen.

⊞ This is the Windows Logo Key on your keyboard. Press this key in combination with other keys to access keyboard shortcuts. Press this key by itself to display or hide Start.

When starting and using Word, Excel or PowerPoint without a document, the start screen provides options for creating a new document or opening an existing document. If you have a file open already, CLICK FILE, NEW or CLICK FILE, OPEN for similar options.

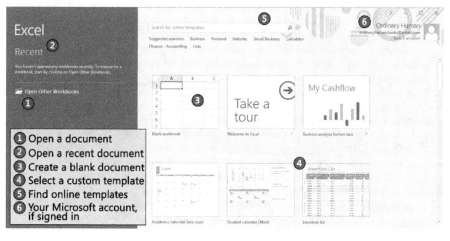

① Open a document
② Open a recent document
③ Create a blank document
④ Select a custom template
⑤ Find online templates
⑥ Your Microsoft account, if signed in

You don't have to use a Microsoft account with Office 2019. However, having one allows you to save and share your documents online for access by other people, or on other devices. A Microsoft account also allows you to install and use Office add-ins, such as a dictionary or consistency checker.

To sign in:

1. Choose File and then Account.

2. CLICK **Sign In**, then follow the instructions for signing in or creating an account.

When you are signed in, you can get add-ins from the Microsoft store. To install add-ins:

1. CLICK INSERT, **Store**.

2. Search for add-ins and CLICK an add-in to view its details page.

3. CLICK TRUST IT.

To use add-ins:

1. CLICK INSERT, .

2. The Office Add-Ins dialog box shows available add-ins.

3. CLICK the add-in to use, then CLICK **Insert**.

Working with the Ribbon

The Ribbon displays along the top of the window in Word, Excel and PowerPoint. Use the tabs to display groups of related commands. Keep in mind some tabs, such as Table Tools and Picture Tools, only appear when you select a table or picture.

CLICK the Show Dialog button in a group to display additional options. For example, CLICK the Show Dialog button in the Font group to display additional font options.

Changing How the Ribbon Displays

While it's handy to have the ribbon open at all times, the ribbon takes up a lot of space and you may want to control its display. You can work with the ribbon in several ways.

- To collapse the ribbon, CLICK ⌃ on the right side of the ribbon.
- To temporarily show a collapsed ribbon, CLICK a tab on the ribbon. You can then select a command.
- Alternatively, show or hide the collapsed ribbon by pressing CTRL + F1.

To keep the ribbon open while you work, pin it:

1. CLICK a tab on the title bar.

2. CLICK 📌 .

Hiding the Ribbon Completely

To completely hide the ribbon:

1. CLICK 🗔 on the right side of the title bar.
2. CLICK Auto-Hide Ribbon.

CLICK in the title bar to display a hidden ribbon or press and hold ALT.

To stop hiding the ribbon:

1. CLICK 🗔 on the right side of the title bar.
2. CLICK Show Tabs or Show Tabs And Commands.

Using the Quick Access Toolbar

The Quick Access toolbar is displayed on the left side of the ribbon.

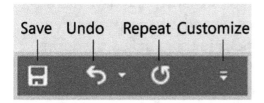

The default options are:

- **Save**   Saves the open document
- **Undo**   Undoes the last action
- **Repeat / Redo**   Repeats or redoes the last action
- **Customize**   Displays options for adding or removing buttons

Any command on any tab or toolbar can be added to quick access. To add a command, RIGHT-CLICK the command on a tab or other ribbon location, then select Add To Quick Access Toolbar.

To remove a command, RIGHT-CLICK the command on the quick access toolbar, then select Remove From Quick Access Toolbar.

Optimizing for Touch UI

You can optimize the ribbon for either mouse and keyboard or touch mode. To add the Touch/Mouse Mode button to Quick Access:

1. CLICK ![icon] on the Quick Access toolbar.
2. CLICK Touch/Mouse Mode.

With the Touch/Mouse button added to Quick Access, CLICK

, then CLICK Touch.

With touch UI mode, commands are larger and have more space between them. Some commands change from using button/drop-down combinations to using only drop-downs.

To use Mouse Mode instead, CLICK , then CLICK Mouse.

Displaying KeyTips

KeyTips are keyboard shortcuts that are displayed when you press the ALT key. Press the ALT key to display KeyTips and letters appear on tab names. To go to the tab, you then press the corresponding key on your keyboard, such as pressing ALT + H to go to the Home tab.

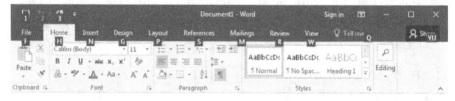

To use KeyTips as shortcuts:

1. Press the ALT key and then press the letter on your keyboard for the tab you want to display.
2. The tab is displayed with KeyTips for menu items. Press the letter on your keyboard for the command you want to use.

Working with Document Windows

Each document you open in an Office application is opened in a separate window.

Opening a New Document Window

Opening a new window opens a blank document in the Office application.

- CLICK View, then CLICK New Window.

Switching Document Windows

Switch
Windows ▾

1. Choose View, then CLICK   .
2. Select the document window to open.

You also can use the Windows taskbar to switch between document windows. CLICK the icon for the Office application on the taskbar, then select the document window to open.

Arranging Document Windows

The windows for an Office application can be opened side by side or cascaded.

- CLICK View, then select Arrange All to arrange windows side by side.
- CLICK View, then select Cascade to cascade windows.

Hiding, Opening and Closing Document Windows

Minimize document window so it's hidden from view (but not closed).

Maximize document window to full screen mode.

Exit full screen mode.

Close a document window. If there are unsaved changes, click Yes to save the changes.

Working with Documents

Use the File menu to manage your documents, including opening, saving, printing, sending via email and closing.

- Open the File menu by choosing File on the ribbon.

- Close the File menu by selecting ![icon], then clicking in the document or selecting a ribbon tab.

Creating a New Document

To create a blank document press CTRL + N. Or:

1. Choose File and then New.
2. Select the Blank template.

Creating a New Document from a Template

1. Choose File and then New.
2. Select the template to use.

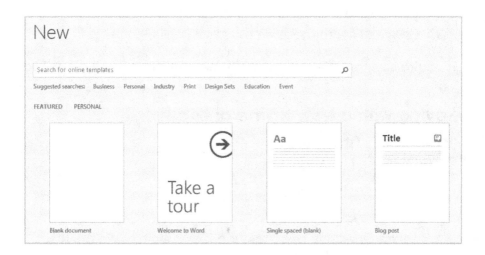

You also can find templates online by searching for the type of document you want to create. To find a template online:

1. Choose File and then New.
2. Type descriptive text in the Search box, then press Enter. Use suggested searches to quickly find a particular type of document, such as a business or personal document.

Opening an Existing Document

1. Choose File and then Open.
2. Select a recently opened document, or:

- Select This PC to open My Documents.
- Select OneDrive or other web locations for files stored online.
- Select Browse to search for the file to open.

3. Select a file, then CLICK Open.

Saving a Document

To overwrite a file that has already been saved:

- CLICK 💾 on the Quick Access toolbar.
- Choose File, then Save or press CTRL + S.

If you're saving a file for the first time, see the next section.

Saving with a New Name or Location

1. Choose File, then Save As.
2. The last used location is selected by default:

- Select This PC to save to a Recent folder, My Documents or Desktop.
- Select OneDrive or other web locations to save online.
- Select Browse to search for the save location.

3. Type a file name, then CLICK Save.

Saving a PDF

The Portable Document Format (PDF) is the format used with Adobe Acrobat and Adobe Reader. After you save a document in an Office format, you can save the document as a PDF.

To create a PDF copy of a document:

1. Choose File, Export, then select

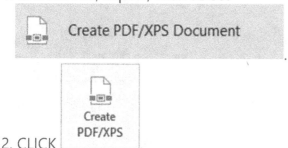

2. CLICK
3. Type a filename, then choose a save location.
4. CLICK Publish.

Viewing and Editing File Properties

All Office documents have properties associated with them, such as the document title, author, tags, and subject. To view document properties, choose File and then Info. File properties are then displayed on the right side of the Info window.

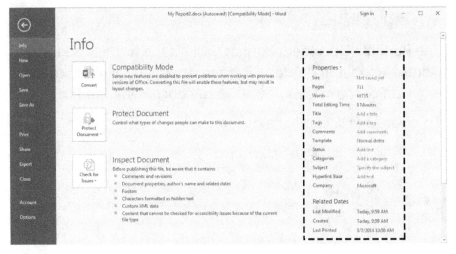

While you are working with the Info window, you can work with document properties in a variety of ways:

- Click Show All Properties to display more document properties.
- Click Show Fewer Properties to display only the basic properties.
- Click the "Add" text to the right of the property name or the actual text you entered to edit the property value.

Documents also have advanced properties associated with them. To view and edit advanced properties:

1. While working with the Info window, CLICK the Properties button.
2. Select Advanced Properties.
3. Enter information about the document on the Summary and Custom tab.

Printing or Previewing a Document

1. Choose File, Print or press CTRL + P.

2. CLICK ◀ or ▶ to view other pages, or press Page Up or Page Down.

3. Show multiple pages by dragging the Zoom In/Out slider to the left or right until the desired number of pages is displayed.

NOTE: CLICK 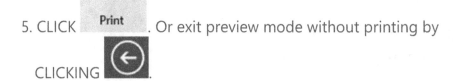 to return to standard page zoom.

4. As necessary, specify the number of copies to print, the printer to use, the pages to print and other print options.

5. CLICK **Print**. Or exit preview mode without printing by CLICKING ⊙.

Sending a Document as an Email Attachment or PDF

1. Choose File, then Share.

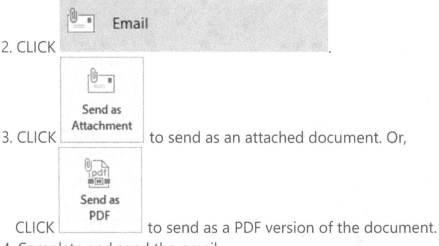

2. CLICK **Email**.

3. CLICK **Send as Attachment** to send as an attached document. Or,

CLICK **Send as PDF** to send as a PDF version of the document.

4. Complete and send the email.

Securing Documents with Passwords

Anyone can open a document and read its contents, which isn't always what you want. To secure a document, you can add a password to lock the file so that only people you give the password to can open it.

Adding a Password to a Document

A document password can be any character string you want to use to protect a document. Passwords are case-sensitive, meaning lowercase letters are different from uppercase letters, and can include numbers as well as other characters, such as !@#$%^&*.

To password-protect a document:

1. Choose File and then Info.
2. Select Protect Document (or Presentation or Workbook).
3. Select Encrypt With Password.

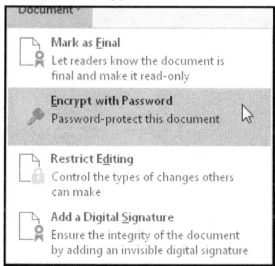

4. In the Encrypt Document dialog box, enter the password that you want to associate with the document, and then CLICK OK.
5. In the Confirm Password dialog box, re-enter the password and then CLICK OK.

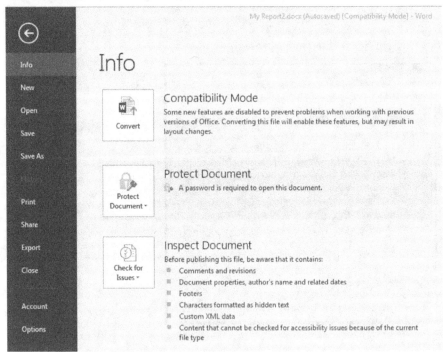

The Info window shows that a password is now required to open the document. Write down the password for the document and store the password in a secure location.

Opening a Password-Protected Document

Once a document is secured with a password, the password is required to open the document. Thus, anyone trying to open the document will see a Password prompt.

When prompted, enter the password, then CLICK OK.

Removing a Password from a Document

If you no longer want a document to be secured with a password, you can remove the password.

1. Open the document that needs its password removed. Choose File and then Info.
2. Select Protect Document (or Presentation or Workbook).
3. Select Encrypt With Password to display the Encrypt With Password dialog box.
4. Delete the password. One way to do this is to click in the Password box and then press the Backspace key until the Password box is empty.
5. Click OK.

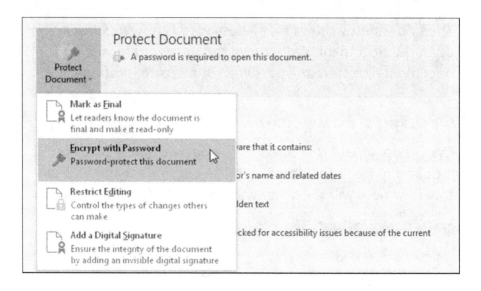

Working with the Status Bar

The status bar is displayed along the bottom of the window. By default, information about the document is displayed on the left and view/layout and zoom options are displayed on the right.

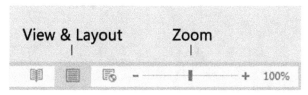

Customizing the Status Bar

RIGHT-CLICK the status bar and select display options to turn them on or off. A checkmark indicates an option is selected.

Zooming In or Out

- DRAG the Zoom slider left to reduce the zoom level (shrink).
- DRAG the Zoom slider right to increase the zoom level (enlarge).
- STRETCH or PINCH.

To use the Zoom dialog box instead:

1. Select View, then CLICK Zoom.
2. Choose a Zoom option.

Changing the View Mode

The view modes determine how you view the document and are optimized for different purposes. With Word, the View layouts are optimized for reading, printing or web viewing modes. With Excel, there are Normal, Page Layout and Page

Break views. With PowerPoint, there are Normal, Slide Sort and Reading views.

To change the view mode:

- CLICK a view button on the Status bar.
- Select View, then choose a view in the Views group.

Managing Text, Pictures and Other Items

You can insert text, pictures and other items into documents. Any inserted item has a related shortcut menu that can be used to modify or format the item.

Shortcut menus display options specific to an item, such as a misspelled word, chart or picture. To use a shortcut menu, RIGHT-CLICK on an item, then select the option from the list, or PRESS AND HOLD, then release when a box appears.

Selecting Text

- DRAG across the text to select. In Excel, first DOUBLE-CLICK to edit the cell contents.
- Hold SHIFT and use the arrow keys. To select words, hold CTRL + SHIFT and use the arrow keys.
- TAP and DRAG to change the start and end points of the selection.
- To select multiple text areas, make a selection, then hold CTRL while making additional selections.

Inserting or Deleting Text

With Excel, you must first DOUBLE-CLICK to edit the cell contents. This isn't necessary with Word or PowerPoint.

To insert text, CLICK where the text is to be inserted, then type.

To delete text, CLICK where the text is to be deleted. If the insertion point is before the text to delete, press the Delete key. If the insertion point is after the text to delete, press the Backspace key.

To delete a large section or paragraph of text, select the text area to delete, then press the Delete or Backspace key.

To replace text, select the text to replace, then type the new text.

Selecting Shapes, Pictures or Excel Cells

- CLICK on a shape, picture or Excel cell.
- To select multiple shapes, DRAG around the shapes.
- To select multiple cells in Excel, DRAG across the cells.
- To select multiple non-adjacent shapes, pictures or cells, hold CTRL while making selections.

While the shape, picture or cell is selected, you can work with it and may find a related management tab is available. RIGHT-CLICK to display management options.

Moving or Copying

1. Select the text, shape, picture, Excel cell or other item to move or copy.
2. To move the item, choose Home, then CLICK Cut or press CTRL + X. To copy the item, choose Home, then CLICK Copy or press CTRL + C.
3. CLICK to place the cursor where you want to move or copy.
4. Choose Home, then CLICK Paste or press CTRL + V.

Some items may have formatting that you want to keep, merge or discard. If so:

1. Select Home, then CLICK Paste.
2. Choose a paste option, such as Keep Source Formatting or Keep Text Only.

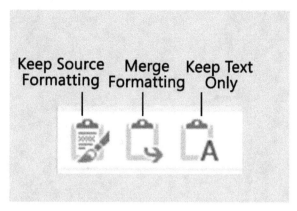

The paste options available depend on the type of item and the Office application you are using.

Dragging and Dropping

1. Select the text, shape, picture, excel cell or other item to move or copy.
2. Move by dragging to the new location. Copy by pressing CTRL while dragging.

Moving Pictures, Shapes, Etc.

To move a picture or other object, DRAG it to a new location. Or press CTRL + X to cut the item from its current location and then press CTRL + V to paste to a new location.

Deleting Shapes, Pictures or Excel Cells

1. CLICK on a shape, picture or Excel cell.
2. Press the Delete or Backspace key.

Using the Clipboard

As discussed previously, you can cut and copy text, pictures and other items by selecting an item and then pressing Ctrl+X or Ctrl+C, or by right-clicking an item and choosing Cut or Copy on the shortcut menu. Once cut or copied, you can paste by pressing Ctrl+V or by right-clicking and choosing Paste.

When you cut and copy text, pictures or other items in the documents you are working with, the items are made available on the clipboard. The clipboard is a special workspace that stores the last 24 items you've cut or copied in any Office application you are working with. For example, you can use the feature to easily copy text or pictures from Word into PowerPoint.

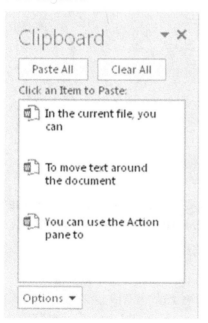

Note the ![icon] icon to the left of the clipboard entry. This tells you where the item came from or the type of item. In the example, the text came from Word. If the text came from another Office app, the icon would be for that app. If the copied item was a picture or other object, the icon would reflect this. For example, the ![icon] icon is displayed with pictures that have been copied to the clipboard.

Displaying the Clipboard

To display the Clipboard task pane, click the Clipboard group button on the Home tab. This button is located to the right of the word Clipboard.

Once you've opened the Clipboard task pane, you can manage the way the Clipboard displays in the future, select Options on the Clipboard Task pane. You can now:

- Turn on or off automatic display of the clipboard by selecting Show Office Clipboard Automatically.
- Turn on or off display of the clipboard when Ctrl+C is pressed twice by selecting Show Office Clipboard When Ctrl+C Is Pressed Twice.

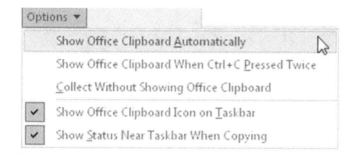

Pasting from the Clipboard

When you are working with the Clipboard task pane, you can paste text, pictures or other items that have been copied by clicking the related entry. Thus, to insert a copied item, you:

1. Click in the document where the item should be added.
2. Then click the related entry in the Clipboard task pane.

Formatting Text

Use formatting to modify the way text looks in your document. Most formatting options are on the Home tab. Remember, selecting cells or shapes then formatting will change all the text within the selected item.

Changing Text Font and Size

1. Select the text or item to change.
2. Choose Home, then select the Font to use.
3. Select a font size or type the size in the combo box provided.

Using Bold, Italic, Underline, Etc.

Text can be styled using bold, italic, underline and strikethrough options. Combine styles as appropriate and necessary.

1. Select the text or item to change.
2. Choose Home, then use the Bold, Italic, Underline and Strikethrough buttons to style the text.

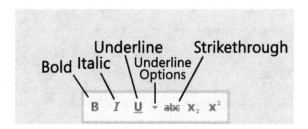

The default underline style is a single line. Click the Underline Options button to select a different underline style, such as dotted underline or dashed underline.

To remove styling:

1. Select the text or item to change.
2. Choose the same styling buttons to remove the previously applied styles.

A common style you may use together is bold italic. To apply this style, you would CLICK the Bold button and then CLICK the Italic button. To subsequently remove this styling, you would select the text, then CLICK the Bold button followed by the Italic button.

Adding Subscript or Superscript

Subscript and superscript are two text effects that you may need to use at work or school. A subscript letter or number is lowered in the text, as with a chemical formula, such as H_2O. A superscript letter or number is raised in the text, as with ordinal numbers like 1st, 2nd and 3rd as well as with scientific and mathematical formulas.

Some Office applications, like Word and PowerPoint, make it easy to add subscript and superscript as related options are in the Font group on the Home tab. To add text with subscript or superscript with these applications:

1. Click the Subscript (X_2) or Superscript (X^2) button on the Home tab to turn on the text effect.
2. Enter the letters or numbers that should be subscript or superscript.
3. Click the Subscript (X_2) or Superscript (X^2) button on the Home tab to turn off the text effect.

You can add subscript or superscript to existing text by selecting it and then clicking X_2 or X^2.

With Excel and other Office applications that don't have subscript or superscript buttons on the Home tab, add text with subscript or superscript by:

1. Press Ctrl+D or click the Font group button on the Home tab.

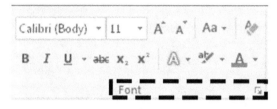

2. Select the Subscript or Superscript checkbox in the Font dialog box to turn on the text effect and then click OK.
3. Enter the letters or numbers that should be subscript or superscript.
4. Press Ctrl+D or click the Font group button on the Home tab.
5. Clear the Subscript or Superscript checkbox in the Font dialog box to turn off the text effect and then click OK.

To add subscript or superscript to existing text (rather than new text):

1. Select the text to which you want to add the text effect.
2. Press Ctrl+D or click the Font group button on the Home tab.
3. Select the Subscript or Superscript checkbox in the Font dialog box to turn on the text effect and then click OK.

Adding Small Caps or All Caps

Other text effects that you may need to use are Small Caps and All Caps. A small cap is a small capital letter that can be used to add styling to titles and other text elements in documents. The

All Caps effect simply capitalizes all letters and can be used anywhere you need text to appear in all capital letters.

To add text formatted with small caps or all caps:

1. Press Ctrl+D or click the Font group button on the Home tab.

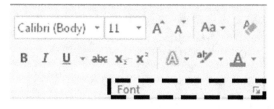

2. Select the Small Caps or All Caps checkbox in the Font dialog box to turn on the text effect and then click OK.
3. Enter the letters or numbers that should be small caps or all caps.
4. Press Ctrl+D or click the Font group button on the Home tab.
5. Clear the Small Caps or All Caps checkbox in the Font dialog box to turn off the text effect and then click OK.

To format existing text as small caps or all caps:

1. Select the text to which you want to add the text effect.
2. Press Ctrl+D or click the Font group button on the Home tab.
3. Select the Small Caps or All Caps checkbox in the Font dialog box to turn on the text effect and then click OK.

Adding Text Colors

1. Select the text or item to modify.
2. Choose Home, then use the Text Color Options button to select the color.

Clicking the Text Color button without using the Options button applies the default or last used color.

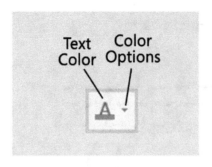

Text Color | Color Options

Changing the Letter Case

Most Office applications, including Word and PowerPoint, provide the Change Case (Aa ▾) button for easily changing the letter case of selected text. These options allow you to quickly apply:

- Sentence case, where the first letter in the first word is capitalized and all other words are lowercase unless they are proper nouns.
- Lowercase, where all letters are lowercase unless they are proper nouns.
- Uppercase, where all letters are always uppercase.

The options also allow you to toggle case or capitalize each word. You use the toggle case option if you accidentally typed with the Caps Lock key turned on. You use capitalize each word when you want the first letter in each word to be capitalized, such as with titles or headings. Keep in mind, however, that the first letter of articles (the, a, an), prepositions (in, of, for ...) and conjunctions (and, but, or, ...) typically aren't capitalized unless they are the first or last word in a title or heading.

To change the letter case:

1. Select the text to format.

2. On the Home tab, click Aa ▾ in the Font group.

Using the Mini Style Toolbar

Use the mini style toolbar to quickly format. This toolbar is displayed beside text, cells or shapes whenever you:

- Select text with a mouse.
- RIGHT-CLICK text, cells or shapes.
- TAP selected items.

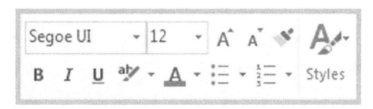

Using the Format Painter

The Format Painter allows you to copy the format of text in a section of your document and paste it onto other text whether in another section of the same document or a completely different document. For example, if you added special formatting to a paragraph of text in Word and wanted to use the same formatting for another paragraph of text, you can use the Format Painter to do this.

You'll find the Format Painter ( ) button in the Clipboard group on the Home tab and on the mini style toolbar.

To copy and apply formatting to one section of text:

1. Click in the text or paragraph where you want to copy the format.
2. Click 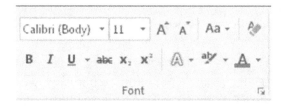 on the Home tab.
3. Drag the pointer across the text to which you want to copy the format.
4. Click another location in the document.

To copy and apply formatting to multiple sections of text:

1. Click in the text or paragraph where you want to copy the format.
2. Double-click on the Home tab.
3. Drag the pointer across the text to which you want to copy the format.
4. Click each location in the document where you want to paste the format.
5. Press Esc or click again to turn off the Format Painter.

Removing All Formatting

Sometimes, you'll want to remove all formatting from a section of text and the Clear All Formatting ( ) button allows you to do this. You'll find this button in the Font group on the Home tab.

Calibri (Body) ▾	11 ▾	A˄ A˅	Aa ▾	ᴬ᷃
B I U ▾ abc x₂ x²	A ▾ ab︣ ▾ A ▾			
	Font			⌐⌐

To clear all formatting from a paragraph of text:

1. Click in the paragraph where you want to remove formatting.

2. Click .

To remove all formatting from a section of text within a paragraph (and not the rest of the paragraph):

1. Select the text where you want to remove formatting.

2. Click .

Adding Pictures, Shapes and SmartArt

The Insert tab is where you'll find options for inserting shapes, pictures and SmartArt.

Inserting Pictures

Office 2019 allows you to add pictures in any compatible file format, including GIF, JPG, BMP, PNG and more.

To add a picture from your computer:

1. Select Insert, CLICK   .
2. Select a picture from your computer, then choose Insert.

To add a picture from an online resource:

1. Select Insert, CLICK Pictures .
2. Search Bing or browse your OneDrive account. Or, CLICK a connected Facebook or Flickr account to browse your other online pictures.
3. Select a picture, then choose Insert.

To format a picture:

1. CLICK the picture to select it.
2. Use Picture Tools, Format to format the picture.

Drawing Shapes

Shapes provide an easy way to add geometric shapes, such as circles, stars, arrows and lines, to your documents.

To draw a shape:

Shapes

1. Select Insert, CLICK .
2. Select a shape to use.
3. CLICK and DRAG where you want to draw the shape.

To format a shape:

1. CLICK the shape to select it.
2. Use Drawing Tools, Format to format the shape.

Using SmartArt

SmartArt helps you add diagrams, organizational charts and other information graphics to your documents.

To add SmartArt:

SmartArt

1. Select Insert, .
2. Use the Choose A SmartArt Graphic dialog box to select the art to use. CLICK a SmartArt to get a description. CLICK a SmartArt, then CLICK OK to add the art.
3. CLICK the placeholder text, then type the desired text.
4. If available, click the picture placeholder, then select the picture to add.

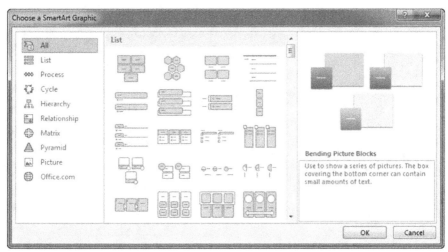

To format art:

1. CLICK the SmartArt to select it.
2. Use SmartArt Tools, Design to modify the art design.
3. Use SmartArt Tools, Format to modify the art format.

Adding Symbols, Special Characters and Hyperlinks

The Insert tab provides options for inserting symbols, special characters and hyperlinks.

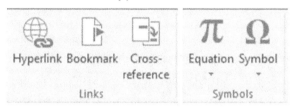

Inserting Symbols and Special Characters

Office applications have either a Symbol Options button on the Insert tab for inserting symbols and special characters:

Or a Symbol button on the Insert tab:

If available, clicking the Symbol Options button displays a dropdown menu of commonly used symbols and special characters, which you can then insert simply by clicking the symbol or character to add.

If the symbol or character you want to use isn't shown, click More Symbols to display the Symbol dialog box, which you can then use to add any listed symbol or special character simply by clicking the symbol or character that you want to use.

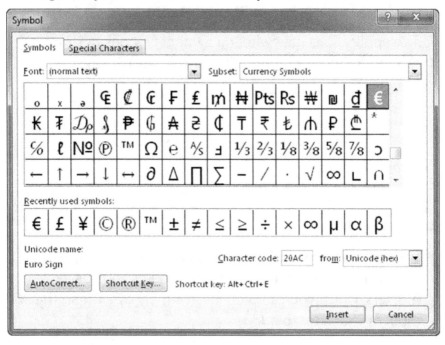

With PowerPoint, Excel and other Office applications that have only a Symbol button, clicking the Symbol button opens the Symbol dialog box directly. In the Symbol dialog box, use the Subset dropdown list to help you find particular types of symbols, such as arrows, currency symbols or dingbats, within the extensive set of available symbols.

To find foreign characters, including characters with umlauts, grave accents or cedillas, select Latin Extended-A or Latin Extended-B as the font subset. Although you typically want the Font dropdown list set to (normal text), you can select Webdings or Wingdings 1, 2, or 3 to view additional special characters that are available with these fonts.

Creating Hyperlinks

You use hyperlinks to link your document to other documents on the Web. A hyperlink provides the web address of a specific page or media so that you or others can click on the hyperlink to access the page or media.

The Hyperlink (Hyperlink) button is on the Insert tab.

To add a hyperlink:

1. Select the text, picture or other item that you want others to click to go to a web page or media on the Internet.

2. On the Insert tab, click Hyperlink .
3. In the Insert Hyperlink dialog box, enter the web page address in the Address box.
4. CLICK OK.

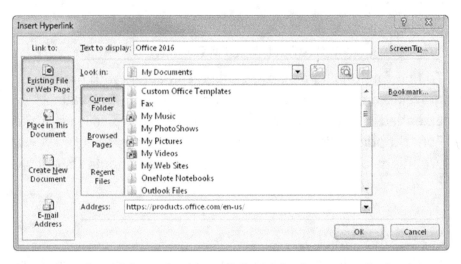

As typing the address for hyperlinks isn't always easy, the Insert Hyperlink dialog box has several options that can help. If you previously browsed to the page in your web browser, you can:

1. Click the Browsed Pages ( ) button in the Insert Hyperlink dialog box.
2. Browsed pages are listed by title or file location. Click an entry in the list to add its address to the Address box.
3. CLICK OK.

If you click the Browse the Web ( ) button, your web browser opens and you can:

1. Go to the web page you want to link to in the web browser.
2. Click the page's address in the web browser to select it.
3. Press Ctrl+C to copy the address.
4. In the Hyperlink dialog box, click in the Address box and then press Ctrl+V to paste the address.
5. CLICK OK.

Changing, Repairing or Removing Hyperlinks

Web addresses can change over time or simply be entered incorrectly in the first place. If you click a hyperlink and nothing happens, the web page or media may no longer be available or may have a new address.

To change or repair a hyperlink:

1. Click in the link and then click Hyperlink (or right-click the link and choose Edit Hyperlink).
2. Use the Edit Hyperlink dialog box to update the hyperlink.
3. CLICK OK.

To remove a hyperlink:

1. Click in the link and then click Hyperlink .
2. In the Edit Hyperlink dialog box, click Remove Hyperlink.
3. CLICK OK.

Alternatively, right-click the link and choose Remove Hyperlink.

Making Changes and Corrections

With Office 2019, common mistakes are fixed automatically while you type, e.g. frmo is changed to from. Some text you type changes to symbols, e.g. (c) changes to ©. AutoCorrect is the feature that performs these changes.

Viewing AutoCorrect Settings

1. Choose File, Options, then select Proofing.
2. CLICK AutoCorrect Options.

- The AutoCorrect checkboxes control basic behavior. Each option with a checkmark is enabled.
- The Replace Text As You Type entries list text that is replaced and shows you the replacement value, e.g. (tm) is replaced with ™.

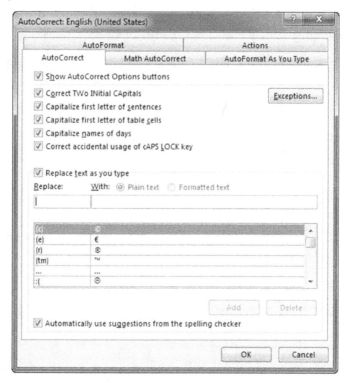

Modifying AutoCorrect Settings

1. Choose File, Options, then select Proofing.
2. CLICK AutoCorrect Options.
3. As appropriate, do the following:

- Clear checkboxes for AutoCorrect options you don't want to use. Select checkboxes for AutoCorrect options you want to use.
- To modify replacement behavior, locate and select an entry to modify, then enter or modify the text in the Replace and With boxes.

Checking Spelling

Word, Excel, and PowerPoint check spelling as you type. A red wavy line shows a spelling error.

To spellcheck an entire document, choose Review and then select Spelling (or Spelling & Grammar with Word).

Correct a mistake, or RIGHT-CLICK the word with the wavy line then:

- If incorrect, choose from the available suggestions.
- If correct for spelling, choose Ignore All or add the word to the Office dictionary by selecting Add To Dictionary.

Checking Grammar

Only Word checks grammar as you type. A blue wavy line shows a grammar error. To grammar check an entire document, choose Review and then select Spelling & Grammar.

Correct a mistake, or RIGHT-CLICK the word with the wavy line then:

- If incorrect, choose from the available suggestions.

- Choose Ignore Once to skip the error.

Using the Dictionary and Thesaurus

Word, Excel, and PowerPoint have a built-in dictionary and thesaurus.

1. Select a word, then choose Review.
2. For definitions, CLICK Smart Lookup, then under Insights, CLICK Define.
3. For synonyms, CLICK Thesaurus.

Undoing or Redoing Actions

Sometimes AutoCorrect will make changes you don't want. If you CLICK or press CTRL + Z immediately after the text is corrected, the change is removed.

Undo is also handy to remove formatting or other changes that you don't want. To undo a change, simply CLICK . To undo other changes, CLICK and choose the changes to undo.

To redo an action, CLICK . This reverses the Undo command. If you used Undo several times, is displayed, allowing you to choose specific changes to redo.

In Excel, you can use and to redo or undo several steps at once.

Repeating Actions

In Word and PowerPoint, changes to when there are no changes to redo. Use to repeat the last action. Alternatively, you can press CTRL + Y to repeat an action.

Managing File Formats

Office 2007 to Office 2019 use the same file format. Here, Office saves files with the file extension docx, pptx or xlsx, e.g. MyReport.docx.

The x in the filename tells you the files are stored as a special type of Zip archive that contains the elements of your document stored in separate files. In the archive, the document itself is formatted using XHTML, an extensible markup language that is based on an open standard.

Opening Files Created in Earlier Versions of Office

Office 2003 and earlier save files with the extension doc, ptt or xls. These files are stored using a proprietary formatting that is exclusive to Microsoft.

In Office 2019, you can open documents using the current or older format. Office 2019 uses a compatibility mode when opening files created with an earlier file format. Features are disabled or modified as necessary to ensure compatibility. Older Office versions also use a compatibility mode when opening newer file formats.

Saving Files Created in Earlier Versions of Office

Documents are saved by default in the format they were created in. You can easily save a document created in the old format with the new format and vice versa, e.g. a doc file can be saved as a docx file or a docx file can be saved as a doc file.

To save a file using a format other than its original format:

1. Choose File and then Save As.

2. Select a save location.
3. Type a file name.
4. Select Save As Type, then choose the type.

Checking Compatibility with Earlier Versions

Although Office 2007 to Office 2019 use the same file format, various features and options are different in each of these versions. These differences mean that sometimes your document won't work as expected in a different Office version.

To determine how your Office 2019 document will work when opened with an earlier version of Office:

1. Choose File and then Info.
2. Select Check For Issues, then select Check Compatibility.
3. To change the version to check, choose Select Versions To Show, then clear or select the checkboxes for the versions.
4. Note any problems, then CLICK OK.

Converting Office 97-2013 Documents

When you open a file created in an earlier version of Office, Office uses compatibility mode to display the document. Documents displayed in compatibility mode use the features and options of the earlier Office version. You can tell a file is in compatibility mode because [Compatibility Mode] is displayed after the file name on the title bar.

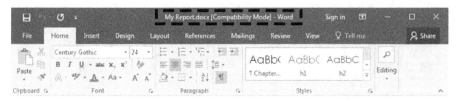

It's important to note that when you convert a file from an earlier version, the file structure is updated as required for Office 2019. This update process may result in some formatting and other changes in the document, especially when converting very early Office files to this latest version.

Converting to Office 2019 File Format

1. Choose File and then Info.
2. Select Convert.
3. When prompted to confirm, CLICK OK.

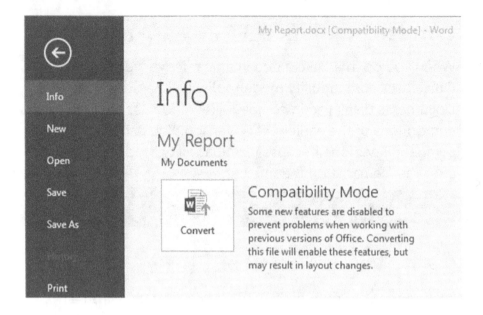

Preventing a File from Being Converted

Sometimes you may not want a document format to be upgraded to the most recent file format, such as when you have specific requirements for documents from your workplace. To prevent a document from being converted to the Office 2019 file format and preserve the current options:

1. Chose File and then Save As.
2. Select More Options.

3. Select Maintain Compatibility With Previous Versions.
4. CLICK SAVE.

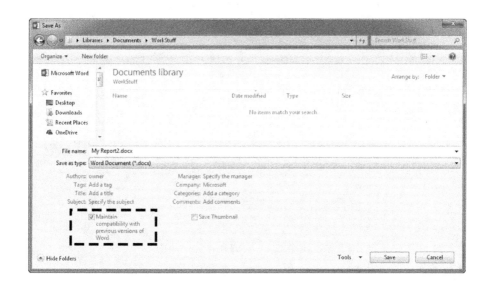

Protecting Documents with AutoRecovery

To help protect your documents and prevent data loss, AutoRecovery is the feature Office 2019 uses to automatically save documents you are working on so that they can be recovered in case Office freezes or your computer fails.

Files saved by Office as part of AutoRecovery are called AutoSave files. Files you save by clicking or using Save As are referred to as the Original files.

The data saved for AutoRecovery isn't necessarily the same data that would be preserved with a full save of a document. For this reason, as you work on documents, you should periodically CLICK to ensure the additions and changes you've made are fully saved.

Configuring AutoRecovery

By default, Office saves AutoRecovery files every ten minutes and keeps that last autosaved version if you close Office without saving. You may want Office to save your changes more frequently, such as every 5 minutes, if you're worried about losing your additions and changes. It's important not to save AutoRecovery information too frequently, however, as this can make your computer sluggish or nonresponsive.

To configure AutoRecovery:

1. Chose File and then Options.
2. In the Options dialog box, select Save.
3. Ensure the Save AutoRecovery Information checkbox is checked.

4. Type a Minutes setting in the Save AutoRecovery Information box.
5. CLICK OK.

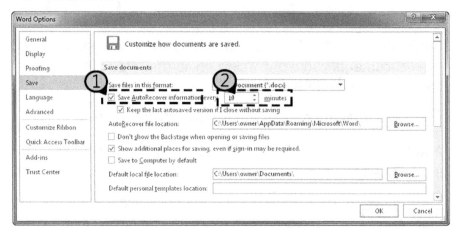

Recovering Documents

Should Office freeze or your computer fail while you are working on documents, you can initiate the document recovery process:

1. Start or restart the Office program you were working with.
2. Open a document or create a new blank document.
3. Office opens the Document Recovery task pane.

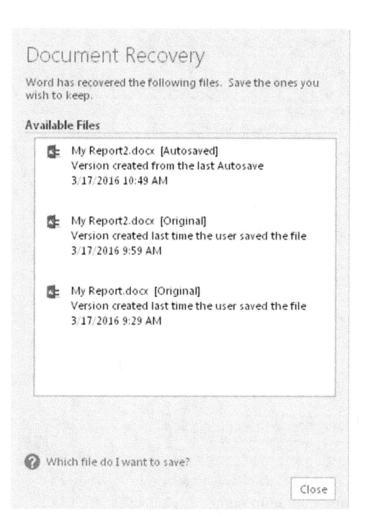

Document Recovery

Word has recovered the following files. Save the ones you wish to keep.

Available Files

My Report2.docx [Autosaved]
Version created from the last Autosave
3/17/2016 10:49 AM

My Report2.docx [Original]
Version created last time the user saved the file
3/17/2016 9:59 AM

My Report.docx [Original]
Version created last time the user saved the file
3/17/2016 9:29 AM

Which file do I want to save?

Close

If you had open files that you were working on when the problem occurred, you'll see a list of those files on the Document Recovery pane. Files are listed with version information, save time and an indicator regarding whether each is an AutoSave or Original file. If a file was repaired because of a problem, you'll see details about the repair operation as well. Click files in the list to display recovery options.

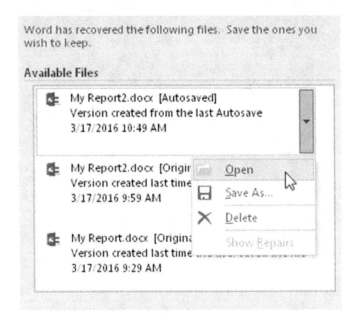

Word has recovered the following files. Save the ones you wish to keep.

Available Files

🗐 My Report2.docx [Autosaved]
Version created from the last Autosave
3/17/2016 10:49 AM

🗐 My Report2.docx [Origir   📁 <u>O</u>pen
Version created last time
3/17/2016 9:59 AM   💾 <u>S</u>ave As...

                            ✕   <u>D</u>elete

🗐 My Report.docx [Origina   Show <u>R</u>epairs
Version created last time
3/17/2016 9:29 AM

To work with the files in the recovery list:

1. Click a file in the list to display options.
2. Choose a recovery option:

- **Open/View**   Opens the file so you can review and work with it. If you want to keep the file, be sure to CLICK 💾.
- **Save As**   Displays the Save As dialog box so you can save the file with a different name. This allows you to keep a copy of the recovered file in case you need it.
- **Delete**   Deletes the AutoRecovery file (and removes the related listing from the Document Recovery pane). Although you may want to delete AutoSave files that aren't needed, only delete Original files when you no longer need the files.
- **Show Repairs**   If a file was repaired, use this option to show the repairs made to the file. You should also closely review the repaired file before saving it, and may also want to save the file with a different file name to ensure the original is available in case you need it.

Commonly Used Office Shortcuts

Bold (On/Off)	CTRL +B
Close Active Widow	CTRL + W
Close Dialog	ESC
Copy selected items	CTRL + C
Cut selected items	CTRL + X
Cycle through open windows	CTRL + TAB
Display Help	F1
Display Ribbon (Show/Hide)	ALT or F10
Find And Replace	CTRL + H
Find	CTRL + F
Insert Hyperlink	CTRL + K
Italic (On/Off)	CTRL +I
New document	CTRL + N
Open a document	CTRL + O
Paste Special	CTRL + ALT + V
Paste the clipboard contents	CTRL + V
Print a document	CTRL + P
Redo or repeat the last action	CTRL +Y

Repeat Find (after closing Find)	SHIFT + F4
Ribbon (Show/Hide)	CTRL + F1
Save As	F12
Save current document	CTRL + S
Select a paragraph	Triple Click
Select a Word	Double Click
Select All	CTRL + A
Selection Pane (Show/Hide)	ALT + F10
Shortcut Menu	SHIFT + F10
Spell Check	F7
Thesaurus	SHIFT + F7
Underline (On/Off)	CTRL +U
Undo the last action	CTRL +Z

Word 2019 Shortcuts

Text Selection Shortcuts

Select a word	DOUBLE-CLICK the word
Select a sentence	CLICK the sentence
Select a paragraph	DOUBLE-CLICK selection area beside the paragraph or TRIPLE-CLICK in paragraph
Select all text	CTRL + A
Make multiple selections	Press CTRL while making additional selections

Special Character Shortcuts

Column break	CTRL + SHIFT + Enter
Ellipsis	ALT + CTRL + period
Line break	SHIFT + Enter
Non-breaking space	CTRL + SHIFT + space
Page break	CTRL + Enter
Copyright symbol	ALT + CTRL + C
Registered trademark symbol	ALT + CTRL + R
Trademark symbol	ALT + CTRL + T

Navigation Shortcuts

Hold SHIFT with any of the navigation shortcuts to select from the current position to that position.

Beginning of document	CTRL + Home
Beginning of line	Home
End of document	CTRL + End
End of line	End
Go to page number	F5
Top of the next page	CTRL + Page Down
Top of the previous page	CTRL + Page Up

View Shortcuts

Outline view	ALT + CTRL + O
Draft view	ALT + CTRL + N
Print preview	ALT + CTRL + I
Print layout	ALT + CTRL + P

Formatting Shortcuts

All capitals (on/off)	CTRL + SHIFT + A
Apply H1 style	ALT + CTRL + 1
Apply H2 style	ALT + CTRL + 2
Apply H3 style	ALT + CTRL + 3
Apply Normal style	CTRL + SHIFT + N
Bold (on/off)	CTRL + B
Change case of letters	SHIFT + F3
Center (on/off)	CTRL + E
Decrease font size by 1 point	CTRL + [
Decrease font size	CTRL + SHIFT + <
Decrease left indent	CTRL + SHIFT + M
Display Font dialog box	CTRL + D
Double underline (on/off)	CTRL + SHIFT + D
Increase font size by 1 point	CTRL +]
Increase font size	CTRL + SHIFT + >
Increase left indent	CTRL + M
Italic (on/off)	CTRL + I

Justify (on/off)	CTRL + J
Left-align (on/off)	CTRL + L
Reveal formatting on paragraphs	SHIFT + F1
Right-align (on/off)	CTRL + R
Small capitals (on/off)	CTRL + SHIFT + K
Underline (on/off)	CTRL + U

PowerPoint 2019 Shortcuts

General Shortcuts

Change case of letters	SHIFT + F3
Collapse paragraph (outline)	ALT + SHIFT + -
Create a new slide	CTRL + M
Decrease font size	CTRL + SHIFT + <
Demote paragraph/bullet	ALT + SHIFT + ←
Display Font dialog box	CTRL + T
Duplicate selected object	CTRL + D
Expand paragraph (outline)	ALT + SHIFT + +
Grid (on/off)	SHIFT + F9
Guides (on/off)	F9
Increase font size	CTRL + SHIFT + >
Line break	SHIFT + Enter
Move to next textbox on slide	CTRL + Enter
Play a slide show	F5
Promote paragraph/bullet	ALT + SHIFT + →

Media Shortcuts

Decrease volume	ALT + Down Arrow key
Increase volume	ALT + Up Arrow key
Jump backward	ALT + SHIFT + ←
Jump forward	ALT + SHIFT + →
Mute (on/off)	ALT + U
Next bookmark	ALT + End
Pause/Play	ALT + P
Previous bookmark	ALT + Home
Stop playing	ALT + Q

Slideshow Shortcuts

Automatic show (on/off)	S or +
Black screen (on/off)	B or period
Change pointer to arrow	CTRL + A
Change pointer to pen	CTRL + P
End show	ESC
Erase screen annotations	E
First slide	Home

Go to a slide number	Press number then Enter
Go to next hyperlink	Tab
Go to previous hyperlink	SHIFT + Tab
Go to the next hidden slide (when pressed on preceding slide)	H
Hide mouse pointer	CTRL + H
Last slide	End
Next slide	Click, spacebar, N, Page Down or Enter
Previous slide	Backspace, P or Page Up
Select hyperlink	Enter
Show all slides	CTRL + S
Show shortcuts	F1
Show taskbar	CTRL + T
White screen (on/off)	W or comma

Excel 2019 Shortcuts

General Shortcuts

Insert worksheet	SHIFT + F11
Function dialog box	SHIFT + F3
Create a table	CTRL + T
Create a new line in cell	ALT + ENTER
Enter the date	CTRL + ;
Enter the time	CTRL + SHIFT + :
Name Manager	CTRL + F3
Create names from row/column labels	CTRL + SHIFT + F3
Edit the active cell	F2
Add/Edit cell comment	SHIFT + F2
Insert chart sheet based on selection	F11
Insert chart	ALT + F1
Delete selected cells	CTRL + -
Insert blank cells	CTRL + SHIFT + +

Special Character Shortcuts

Press ALT and use numeric keypad. These also work for Word and PowerPoint.

¢	ALT + 0162
£	ALT + 0163
¥	ALT + 0165
€	ALT + 0128

Selection Shortcuts

All comments	CTRL + SHIFT + O
All objects (with an object selected)	CTRL + SHIFT + spacebar
Area around active cell	CTRL + SHIFT + * or CTRL + SHIFT + spacebar
Array containing active cell	CTRL + /
Cells containing formulas that directly or indirectly reference the active cell	CTRL + SHIFT + }
Cells containing formulas that directly reference active cell	CTRL +]

Cells that don't match value in active cell (with column selected)	CTRL + SHIFT + |
Cells that don't match value in active cell (with row selected)	CTRL + \
Cells directly or indirectly referenced by formulas in the selection	CTRL + {
Cells directly referenced by formulas in the selection	CTRL + [
Column	CTRL + spacebar. Or CLICK the column heading
Named range	CLICK the name from the Name Box list
Range	Select a range, press CTRL and select additional ranges
Row	SHIFT + spacebar. Or CLICK the row heading
Visible cells in current selection (not hidden cells)	ALT + ;
Worksheet	CTRL + A

Navigation Shortcuts

Hold SHIFT with any of the navigation shortcuts to select from the current position to that position.

Beginning of current row	Home
Cell A1	CTRL + Home
Go to Cell	F5
Last filled cell (or next filled cell if in blank cell) in any direction	CTRL + arrow key
Last used column/row	CTRL + End
Next unlocked cell (in protected worksheet)	Tab
Next worksheet	CTRL + Page Down
Previous worksheet	CTRL + Page Up
Screen down	Page Down
Screen left	ALT + Page Up
Screen right	ALT + Page Down
Screen up	Page Up

Fill, Formatting & Formula Shortcuts

Format Cells dialog box	CTRL + 1
Formula palette (after entering function name in formula)	CTRL + A
Apply the Currency format	CTRL + SHIFT + $
Apply the Date format	CTRL + SHIFT + #
Apply the general number format	CTRL + SHIFT + -
Apply the Number format	CTRL + SHIFT + !
Apply the Percentage format	CTRL + SHIFT + %
Apply the Time format	CTRL + SHIFT + @
Copy formula from cell above	CTRL + SHIFT + '
Copy value from cell above	CTRL + SHIFT + "
Fill down	CTRL + D
Fill right	CTRL + R
Fill selection with current entry	CTRL + Enter
Hide columns	CTRL + 0 (zero)
Hide rows	CTRL + 9

Insert the AutoSum formula	Alt + =
Outline border	CTRL + SHIFT + &
Paste defined name into formula	F3
Remove outline border	CTRL + SHIFT + _ (underscore)
Unhide columns (with cells that include the hidden items selected)	CTRL + SHIFT +)
Unhide rows (with cells that include the hidden items selected)	CTRL + SHIFT + (

Index

Thank you...

Thank you for purchasing this book. If you enjoyed this book and learned something from it, I hope you'll take a moment to write a review. Your reviews will help to ensure I can keep writing. If you have comments for me, a wish list for additions or feedback about a topic you'd like me to write about next, contact me by sending an email to:

OrdinaryHuman.Books@gmail.com

More Books...

Ordinary Human is hard at work on other books for Microsoft products. If you'd like to see a book for a particular product, let us know!

3rd Edition

Windows 10
for Beginners

The Premiere User Guide for Work, Home & Play

Cheat Sheets Edition: Hacks, Tips, Shortcuts & Tricks.

Standard Ordinary Human

Solutions & Training, 20-year Microsoft Veteran

Notes...

Notes...

Notes...

www.ingramcontent.com/pod-product-compliance
Lightning Source LLC
LaVergne TN
LVHW051745050326
832903LV00029B/2725